Myths and Leg[illegible] Cheshire and the Moorlands
~
a cabinet of curiosities

Doug Pickford

Published by
Sigma Leisure, 1 South Oak Lane, Wilmslow, Cheshire SK9 6AR

British Library Cataloguing in Publication Data
A CIP record for this book is available from the British Library.

ISBN: 1-85058-274-2

Typesetting and Design by
Sigma Hi-Tech Services Ltd

Printed by
Manchester Free Press

Dedicated to
"William, Douglas and Ginger" who set off in search of an adventure.

Acknowledgments
Thanks to Gerald Henshall, Tony Carter and John Mountain for photographic help and Mike Oldham for the diagrams concerning the Abbey Ley. Thanks to Charles for his dowsing ability.

CONTENTS

INTRODUCTION

What is this book all about?

A good question. In a nutshell, it's about the wonderful area around and between Macclesfield and Leek which, because it embraces not one, not two but three counties, it has no overall identity or description. So I've given the area the name "Land of the Three Shires" (where Cheshire, Staffordshire, and Derbyshire meet) as a focal point. This bleak stretch of moorland high up in the hills was the scene of some strange happenings centuries ago.

The book is also about the strange and the unusual within this area. If they have to be labelled or defined then perhaps supernatural may suffice for parts. Further, I hope it explains why certain places are what they are and I hope it encourages readers to visualise the wealth of untapped history there is just waiting, like King Arthur's Knights under The Edge, to emerge. The clues are all around and are obvious and I offer my own solutions. You may very well have solutions of your own, and if so, I would love to hear them.

My family has lived in these parts for centuries in the hills above Macclesfield and Leek so perhaps there is, not surprisingly, an inborn affinity with the place as far as I am concerned. I live and work in the area and always asking the question "Why", you will perhaps appreciate the reasons for this book. I hope this Cabinet of Curiosities encourages questions.

I've commenced this book with a look at Rushton Spencer and its environs, for a variety of reasons. It's on the borders of Staffordshire and Cheshire and it has the River Dane, a waterway that figures prominently within, running by. It has also, many magical and mystical connections with days long gone.

As we wander around the area on a voyage of exploration, I hope it becomes obvious that much is inter-related and that both Macclesfield and Leek, although standing some 13 miles apart, are closer than those miles suggest.

Land of the Three Shires

In 1621 it was recorded that at the site of the meeting place of the three shires there were three boundary stones. Today, they have gone.

Of Three Shires Head strange tales are told
Of coiners, thieves, and bandits bold,
Who long defied the country reeve
By hiding in some neighbouring greave;
Or, crossing o'er the border stream,
Which here with rapid waters teem,
His jurisdiction might defy
And their nefarious burdens ply.

Walter Smith, 1923

Astride one of the north western boundaries of the ancient kingdom of Mercia is a district now taking in parts of the counties of Cheshire, Derbyshire and Staffordshire. It is the Land of the Three Shires and it is a delight.

At the time of the Roman invasions both Leek and Macclesfield were part of the land of the Cornavi tribe. The name *Macclesfield* implies a boundary, a mark in the field, and Leek is old Norse for a brook or a stream. Geographically, it is an area of stark contrasts. Lush green meadowland, soggy and foggy marshes, ragged outcrops, pine forests, old oaks and bleak moorland all compete for space.

Although much has been written of the area's history, there is still an untapped source of wealth. There have been dedicated prospectors who have searched for its ancient riches over the years – they have dug deeply and struck several veins, but a great deal remains unearthed.

Our Land of the Three Shires has many sites that were holy before Christendom took over these Isles. Legends of times long gone and reminders of Earth Knowledge remain. Magical and mystical places abound and the unusual can still be accepted as matter of fact.

And there is more.

This was a land where kings and queens were entertained; where noblemen built great halls; where influential holymen built on sites worshipped by pagan man; where Celtic initiates demanded human sacrifice; where waters contained sources of terror and promises of healing and, more recently, where people lived in fear of black witchcraft.

And far more.

From high Cloud to lofty Tor, from low-lying Lud Church to the mystical hills of the Roaches, there is much exploration to be done.

Hugh's Bridge

On the A523 Macclesfield to Leek road, on the Cheshire/Staffordshire border

About halfway between Macclesfield and Leek on the Turnpike road whereon heavy traffic thunders twixt Manchester and Derby the counties of Staffordshire and Cheshire are divided by the River Dane.

Leek is in the northernmost part of Staffordshire but there is little doubt that at one time it was part of Cheshire, owned by the Earls of Chester for centuries. The main road crosses the river at Hug Bridge, a corruption of Hugh's Bridge, once owned by Hugh Despencer.

The Despencers came over with William the Conqueror, and their name implies they were medics or dispensers of medicine, arms or rations. For their services during and after the invasion – and specifically it is believed for the way they helped subdue the people of Macclesfield, Leek and surrounding areas after the Conquest – they were given much land which they held in Knights Service. This meant the land was owned by the Earl of Chester but held by the head of the Despencer clan who was to follow the Earl to war with a certain number of foot soldiers all properly equipped should the occasion demand. The occasion did demand several times with battles against the invading Welsh and with some Crusades undertaken by the Norman Earls.

In some manuscripts they are known as the Le deSpencers and the most oft recorded are Hugh Despencer the Elder and Hugh Despencer the Younger. Both were executed in 1326 by Queen Isabella and her lover Roger Mortimer for the father and son were unpopular favourites of Edward II. Hugh the Younger was as avaricious and wicked as his father and greatly influenced the homosexual Edward. Before their executions they were disinherited and exiled and The Younger became a pirate in the English Channel before returning to power when the Elder was created Earl of Winchester. However the King's wife and her lover took control again and executed them both in most horrifying manner.

Undoubtedly, payment was required to cross this bridge although the major road between Leek and Macclesfield in those times was not the Turnpike one of today but followed a line north to south from Sutton through Wincle to Gun Hill and down to Leek via the Abbey of Dieulacresse.

Hugh's Bridge must have been an important crossing, however and it is recorded that in 1620 the wooden bridge was destroyed in a flood and some two years later the Cheshire Justices rebuilt their half in stone. The Staffordshire portion was left to the township of Rushton Spencer and still consisted of "long, tottering and loose poles" in 1624 when the township appealed for a grant from the Staffordshire justices.

Hugh's or Hug Bridge

Rushton – Hamlet of Rushes

Four miles from Leek on the A523

Just beyond Hug Bridge is Rushton, the Hamlet of Rushes. More particularly, it is Rushton Spencer, the Hamlet of rushes of the Despencers.

Above Rushton, on a hill, there stands alone the church of St Laurence watching over the area, symbolic of the manner in which it has watched over the spiritual lives of Rushton residents for centuries past.

On a winter's morning the valley is often completely enveloped in a mist but, peeping out above the greyness, the church and graveyard can be seen – an eerie sight which calls to mind angels sitting on a cloud. The church stands just off the ancient highway from Congleton to Leek and to the Cistercian Abbey of Dieulacresse, still known as Earlsway – the way of the Earls of Chester.

The need for a church in the rural area was realised by the monks of Leek as long ago as the year 1200 and, as we shall see in proceeding pages, they did what their counterparts in many areas did and founded a Christian church on a pagan site. There was a stone on the top of the hill which the monks knew was worshipped by followers of the old religions and so they uprooted it and rolled it down the hill.

In "Stone Field" just below, the stone came to rest and it took the name of Satan's Stone or the Devil's Stone.

Satan's Stone

Take the footpath from Rushton Church south towards the disused railway line

But, as in so many cases of this kind, there is a legend which surrounds the stone. It is a legend not confined to Rushton – it is common throughout England and Wales. The legend avers that when the foundations of the church were being laid, Satan repeatedly caused the stones to be moved and himself carried many of them down into the marsh. But the builders persevered, themselves hewing and transporting larger and larger stones until at last, the Devil gave up his fight.

His last stone was, says the legend, the one still to be seen until recently in the field. Marks on the stone are said to indicate where Satan sat down to rest and grooves are said to be the marks caused by his apron strings as they burned into the stone. Today there is still a permanent indication of the pagan site on top of the hill for the entrance to the church is heralded by two ancient rounded stones.

Originally the church was wattle and daub but then had wooden walls and was followed by stone walls. Under the old flagged floor lie the remains of many parishioners and what else lies there must be left to the imagination but legend states that there was once a secret passage leading from the church to a farmhouse in the adjacent hill.

We shall hear more of secret passages later.

Rushton's ancient Church, where the monks rolled the Devil's Stone down the hill.

Rushton, the Hamlet of Rushes, early this century

RUSHTON

WELL-DRESSING & HORTICULTURAL SOCIETY.

:-: THE ANNUAL :-:

HORTICULTURAL SHOW

will be held in the School Field on

THURSDAY, AUGUST 7TH, 1924,

and will be opened at 3-15 by the

Hon. T. P. Cholmondley

(Unionist Candidate for the Leek Division),

The Well-Dressing and Crowning of the Rose Queen

[Miss MARY EARDLEY], attended by her Maids of Honour, at 2-30 and 7 o'clock.

Maypole and Country Dances
under the Direction of the Misses Simpson & Goldstraw.

The Address at the Well will be given by the REV. J. S. MORRIS, Vicar of Endon.

Exhibition of Botanical Specimens by Mr. Jos. Austin, Leek.

THE CONGLETON TOWN PRIZE BAND

will play Selections and for Outdoor Dancing.

OPEN WALKING MATCH (about Six Miles).

Prizes, 25s., 15s., 10s.

OPEN SPORTS commencing at 4-30, and LOCAL SPORTS at 7-30, after the Maypole Dancing. Entries for Sports close August 5th.

Punch and Judy and Conjuring by Prof. Johnson. Swing-boats, Cocoanut Shies and other Amusements.

First Prize in Open Sweet Pea Class, 30/-. Entries to A. Knight or A. Gratton, Hon. Secs.

TEAS & REFRESHMENTS by Hagston's, Boro' Cafe, Congleton. All Teas Guaranteed, and Unlimited Supply.

ADMISSION TO SHOW & SPORTS: 1/2 including tax, Children under 12, 6d.

A DANCE will be held the same Evening in the SCHOOLS, from 9 to 1 o'clock. Admission One Shilling.

Late Trains will leave Rushton for Leek and the Potteries and Macclesfield (See Company's Bills). Cheap Bookings.

ATLAS PRINTING WORKS, Sports Printers, Derby Street, Macclesfield

Mystic Waters – Wells and Well Dressing

Today, the ceremony of well dressing is a huge tourist industry in the Peak District attracting people from far and wide. It is, like so many things, a throwback to Celtic times when magical properties were associated with the spurting wells. Along came the Christians and gave the wells Christian names after Saints. Now, the Church plays a prominent part in well dressing ceremonies.

In our area twixt Macclesfield and Leek there is no survivor of the past. Only Endon, four miles outside Leek on the road to the Potteries now has a well dressing ceremony.

But our tiny Rushton carried on the tradition of well dressing until the 1920s. Why it stopped I have been unable to ascertain, but I have had the pleasure of talking to one of the last surviving Well Dressing Queens. And it was interesting to note that Rushton carried on another Pagan ceremony during the well dressing – that of Maypole dancing.

St Helen's Well at Rushton Spencer lies just off the main road. From Macclesfield, the highway takes a sharp right hand at the Royal Oak and many motorists now use the old road "over the top" here as a short cut, returning to the main road two or so miles beyond. Just up this road a few hundred yards on the right can still be seen St Helen's Well, although at the time of writing, it was overgrown and almost unrecognisable.

A former Rushton Vicar, the Rev. William Melland, maintained it was St Daniel's Well and not St Helen's, but there is no support for this. This Well, it is said, would suddenly dry up – especially in May when, after the winter thaw, the springs should be full of water. This foretold evil, the Rushton folk feared. The timing (at the beginning of May) connects with the Celtic feast on May 1st of Beltaine.

It is recorded that the well ran dry before the Civil War, when Charles 1st was beheaded, the famine of 1670, the Gunpowder Plot, and in more recent times the outbreak of the First World War and the death of Edward VII. I have been unable to discover what happened before the outbreak of the Second World War.

In later years, Rushton's Well Dressing was held in August and was more of a village fete than anything, with a horticultural show and maypole and country dancing. An address was given at the well by a clergyman and the Queen was carried to the field where the show was held above the shoulders of several strong men.

Rushton's Queen of 1924, Miss Mary Eardley. The ceremony was stopped some short while after this one.

The "dressed" well, a Christianised relic of pagan times. The site of the well at Rushton is much neglected, at the time of writing.

A Clergyman leads the Queen after the well dressing ceremony.

Dancing around the Maypole, 1910.

Turned in His Grave

We cannot leave Rushton without reference to the gruesome fate which befell a young man in the late 18th century.

On a gravestone at St Laurence's Church there is inscribed in English, Latin and Greek, the following: "Memento Mori (Be mindful of death), Thomas, son of Thomas and Mary Meaykin. Interred July 16th 1781 aged 21 years. As a man falleth before wicked men, so fell I.Bia Thanates (Death of violence)".

This young man went to Stone in Staffordshire from Rushton to seek his fortune. An unlikely place at first glance but it was riding the crest of the wave of the Industrial Revolution at that time. He became a houseboy to an un-named apothecary and, we are told, became affectionate with the master's daughter. Quite suddenly, young Thomas became ill and equally suddenly he was pronounced dead and was buried in St Michael's churchyard at Stone on July 16th 1781.

Thomas's favourite pony found its way to the churchyard and began to scrape on his grave and this strange behaviour started tongues wagging but it was to be 12 months later before an exhumation was carried out. It was to be discovered that Thomas (who had been buried face upwards) was lying face down.

His master never stood trial for murder but the rumour was, quite obviously, that a drug had been administered to the youth.

His remains were taken to Rushton and re-buried on July 17th 1782, the wrong way round to prevent his ghost wandering.

More about wells . .

The Egg Well

One and a half miles from Leek on the A523 to Ashbourne, turn right at Bradnop crossroads and follow the minor road for about one mile.

Just outside Leek, on the road to Ashbourne, is the village of Bradnop and there can be found a well used to be venerated for its healing properties and known as The Egg Well.

It may be known as the Egg Well because of its oval shape. However, ancient Druidic Lore often refers to eggs in connection with healing rites and they believed the universe was hatched from two eggs. The stone basin of the Egg Well has an inscription surrounding it. It says, "Renibus et Speni Cordi, Jecorique Medetur, Mille Maelis Prodest Ista Salubris Aqua". This translates: "The liver, kidneys, heart's disease these waters remedy, and by their healing powers assuage full many a malady".

Today the well is surrounded by a modern brick structure and a glance as its waters would quickly warn against trying its mystic properties.

Petrifying Well

On the high road between the Mermaid Inn and Bottom House

Along an ancient salt and pack horse way following a moorland ridge out of Leek, at Morridge, there are two small wells or springs. These have petrifying properties, that is: the water contains calcium carbonate, and when an object is left in the water for some period of time, it is hardened due to a coating of lime and gives the impression of being made of stone.

Wishing Well

We shall be discussing Alderley Edge in much more detail later, but we must mention in this section the Wishing Well on the Edge. It is known also as the Wizard's Well. By rocky outcrops the water runs into a trough made of stone. Inscribed above it is: "Drink of this and take thy fill for the water falls by the wizard's will".

It has obvious connections with the famous legend of Merlin and, I fancy, was inscribed as a romantic whimsy within the past 150 years.

Macclesfield and Leek had many wells, they were needed to satisfy the needs of the inhabitants. One well in Macclesfield that was said to have certain healing properties was St Ann's Well at Park Lane and the stone from atop this was kept at the West Park for many years along with the market cross and the stocks. The market cross has now been placed in front of the Parish Church, although not in its original position which was in front of the Guild Hall (Town Hall) and also seen are the town's stocks (a victim of the War Effort) and a stone from the Macclesfield Castle.

Both children and adults are often encouraged to participate in maypole dancing. The church has seen this as harmless for many years and perhaps few churchpeople nowadays realise the pagan significance of the ceremony. This picture shows the maypole dance on Hurdsfield Vicarage lawn around the year 1910.

Saltways, Hollow Ways and Earls' Ways

Along the Congleton to Rushton Spencer road is a house called Earlsway House. Further on, a public house is known as The Crown. These are two remnants of one of the oldest thoroughfares known in the district. It continues out towards Derbyshire, and undoubtedly is named after the Earls of Chester.

There are two reasons for this road. One is that it could pre-date the earls and be an ancient salt road, from the salt pans of Cheshire out to the Peak District and beyond. Another is that it was the route the Earls of Chester and their retinues took to visit their lands in the area and, in particular, the Abbey just north of Leek where the White Monks of the Cistercian Order had been brought for safe keeping away from the marauding Welsh.

The road under the Earlsway can be traced from Congleton where it comes into Staffordshire from Cheshire. It is recorded in a perambulation of 1595 as passing Earlsway House at Rushton, five miles west of Leek. From this point the course appears to take a south easterly direction and has probably been incorporated into the later road plan. The name is found again beyond Leek, at Caldon, where popularly called Yearlsway (Ye Earlsway) it is applied to a short stretch of minor road running south to Caldon from the Crown Inn at Waterhouses. At Caldon it was known as the "via comitis" around the year 1200.

The monks of Dieulacresse Abbey sent much wool over to Chester so that it could be exported and, undoubtedly, the Earlsway was the route on which great trains of packhorses would wend their way.

But there was another way the monks would take as well, and this one was to the north, through Macclesfield. They owned land for grazing at Monks Heath and at Alderley Edge as well as around the Leek area and Swythamley Hall is on the site of a Grange belonging to the Abbey.

This road to the north was in parts known as The Hollow Way and went through Gun Gate over Gun Hill and by Bearda Hill at Swythamley past Swythamley Hall to Danebridge, passing Wincle Grange where fellow monks from Combermere Abbey resided and on to Bennetshill past the prominent feature of Cleulow Cross then down to Sutton and to Macclesfield.

Two trackways, both ancient in their own right. Top is the Congleton Road at Macclesfield, and the other is Prestbury Road at Upton.

Going south from the abbey the road went through Haregate.

This road was the major artery between Macclesfield and Leek for countless years. It was a road used for commerce – there was much travel between the two market towns – and it was used as a salt way and as an iron way, taking iron from the Peak.

Bonnie Prince Charlie took this route with his army as he marched south to claim the Crown of England, passing the Ship Inn on the way down to the River Dane and stopping to rest at Swythamley Hall.

The Royal Pub on the Earl's Way .... The Crown

"Now Thus"

From Wincle go over the Dane towards Staffordshire, fork left at Bearda Hill, and Swythamley is on the left.

There is a story told of the Squire of Swythamley in those days, a Sir Philip Trafford, who upon hearing of the Pretender's journey disguised himself as a peasant and set about flaying corn. When the Pretender's army arrived, all he would say was "Now thus" and he was unharmed. Commemorating this, the Trafford motto is "Now Thus".

Philip Trafford was from Chorley, near Wilmslow, who went to live at Swythamley Grange around the year 1585. The Traffords or de Traffords originated in Lancashire but held land at Wilmslow by Knights Service, by which they had to find men to make fast the deer in the Forest of Macclesfield for the Earl of Chester's hunting. Philip and wife Hellene were both buried at Chorley so it is obvious that is where their allegiance lay and it is quite likely they were given Swythamley after the Dissolution of the Monasteries.

Leeks's Great Carriers' Road

In the year 1749 an indictment was made against the inhabitants of Leek and Onecote for not repairing "A great carriers road", chiefly used by packhorses carrying salt from the Cheshire Wyches into the Peak and Derbyshire and bringing back malt into Cheshire. This road, it is said, crossed the north of the county from west to east with Congleton and Winster in Derbyshire as terminals. The route through the Staffordshire Moorlands was stated to be from Meerbrook through Middle Hulme fold and then over Blackshawe Moor and up Stonycliff to Blackmere House (now the Mermaid Inn) on Morridge or Morredge. The track then led down the eastern slopes of Morridge to Warslow and probably carried on over the River Dove at Hartington.

The Prosecution Brief mentions that "upon a moderate calculation above 100 packhorses loaded with salt pass weekly through the road." The ascent of Morridge from Blackshaw Moor was so steep that 40 years before "some of the inhabitants of Tetsworth (Tittersworth) made a stone causeway down the bank and several of the carriers contributed towards it . . . to prevent their cattle and goods being damaged and for the sake of having a tolerable road".

The Mermaid on the Drovers' Road

Take the Leek to Buxton A53 then, four miles out, turn right just before the Winking Man public house, follow the B-road to the right.

Blackmere House, built on the great drovers' road over the bleak Staffordshire moorlands, later became the Mermaid Inn.

Nearby stands a pool, known as Mermaid's Pool which is said to be bottomless and over which no birds fly. A mermaid inhabits the pool, the story says, and lures travellers to the death in the murky waters.

The waters of the pool are indeed murky and I have never seen a mermaid. Indeed, I wonder why a mermaid – an inhabitant, so they say, of La Mer, the sea, should want to be in a small pool on a bleak moorland. The answer is obvious. Mermaid is but a corruption of "Meer or Mere Maid" and the earliest traditions of that desolate spot undoubtedly referred to a Maiden of the Mere, especially the Black or Bleak Mere of that area.

Pott Shrigley's Salt Way

One mile north of Bollington.

One of the oldest Salt Ways in the country runs through Pott Shrigley, just north of Macclesfield.

At Pott Shrigley Church, below The Nab, it is possible to walk to a now disused quarry at the foot of Andrew's Knob and then to Brink Farm and the track that wends its way across Bakestonedale Moor.

This paved ridgeway route forms part of a trackway which is believed to have carried on to Scotland. If this is so, it was once one of the major arteries of the British Isles.

On this road are twin stone shafts called the Bowstones and further along there are almost an identical pair of stones known as Robin Hood's Picking Rods. More of these later.

Pott Shrigley, the quaint village on the line of the ancient track. This picture was taken early this century.

Crosses and Circles of Stone

Stones were items of reverence to the ancients. In some stones, followers of the Old Religion believed their gods resided and others, especially those known as the Initiates, were able to receive energy from them. Some people even today can tune in to certain stones and feel a force, rather like an electric current, coming from them. I have known someone to be knocked over by a power of some description coming from a stone standing on Bosley Cloud, which we shall look into later.

The Bowstones name is now spoken as in "Bow and Arrow", but at these stones, the ancients would bow their heads in reverence and so, at one time were known as Bow Stones, as in "Bow to the Queen".

There is an idea that the Bowstones were used to sharpen arrows for archer's bows, but I would merely ask why archers would travel all the way there to sharpen their weapons. There must have been easier ways!

Clulow Cross

On the Sutton to Wincle road behind the Fourways Diner.

The old Macclesfield to Leek road passes Clulow or Cluelow Cross. But what is this stone pillar, now hidden by a plantation of trees?

A theory is that it was erected by the monks of Dieulacresse as a road marker and there is no doubt that, when coming up from the valley of the Dane the pillar would have been seen by travellers. Equally interesting is the fact that at Monks Heath, where these self-same monks grazed sheep, the cross (or nowadays the trees that surround it) can be seen from a tumulus in a field by the crossroads, which is supposedly the burial mound of a Roman soldier.

This wayside cross, once so common, is on the summit of an artificial mound of earth taken, said Dr Sainter in his 19th century "Scientific Rambles Around Macclesfield" from the adjacent beds of soil and rock. This mound or tumulus is 250 feet in diameter, 25 feet in height.

The learned doctor suggested that, although the cross was erected by the wayside, it was not there simply as a marker, but as a pointer to what was underneath. He says the site was of some importance in a military point of view in Celtic, Roman – British and Anglo Saxon times, since from its elevated and commanding position, it embraces a comprehensive range of other eminences from which signals could be exchanged during warlike times; and likewise to the north west there is a wide and expansive view. From the east it was unapproachable on account of an extensive morass. He implies something or someone important lies under it.

The name comes from *clu, clud,* or *clough* (Anglo Saxon) meaning a rocky district and *low* (Anglo Saxon) meaning a rounded hill or barrow. Descending from here to Wincle and within a few yards of the Ship Inn there is a stile or footpath that leads across two fields to Bartomley Farm where there has been unearthed gold rings and chains. These were either Celtic or Saxon.

What Dr Sainter did not say much about was a fact I immediately noticed when I visited Cluelow Cross, by kind permission of the farmer. (I must point out here that the Cross is on private land and permission must be sought before paying a visit).

The fact is this – the cross or pillar is almost exactly the same shape and size with exactly the same markings as the ancient pillars which now stand in West Park in Macclesfield and also a cross known as a Saxon Cross in the graveyard at Leek Parish Church. There is virtually nothing to tell them apart.

Those in Macclesfield's West Park came to the park from Ridge Hall and a former local historian Isaac Finney suggested they were originally at Wincle Grange. On the dissolution of Combermere Abbey, Wincle Grange was sold to George Cotton, Esquire, in 1541 and subsequently passed into the possession of the Leghs of Ridge.

Wincle had remained in the hands of the Earl of Chester until the end of the 12th century, when Earl Randle Blundeville granted to the monks of Combermere Abbey, near Nantwich, one caracute of land in the Forest of Macclesfield in a place called Winchul.

These Cistercians had neighbours only several miles away – at Dieulacresse.

Another reference made regarding the pillars suggested they had been moved from Ridge Hall Farm "so that they may be preserved from further injury", because they were being used as gateposts and that they were very similar to a stone pillar that has Runic scrollwork on the face of the upper part of the stone.

In a field across the road from Cluelow Cross, an ancient burial mound was investigated by Dr Sainter and others in the late nineteenth century. The interment proved to be that of a child or young person and an urn had been inverted (it was of a Celtic type) and among the burnt bones was found a flint knife and a flint arrow head. The burial lay about three feet below the surface and was surrounded by a stone circle twenty feet in diameter with apparently a headstone four feet in height and the same in breadth placed not in the centre of the circle but between two and three feet on one side of it, northwards. Directly opposite the headstone the circle was entered northward by a short avenue of stones; a line of stones also ran up to the circle in an oblique curve.

In an adjoining field southwards, there is to be seen the remains of some small stone circles and square enclosures and at a short distance north east is, in a hollow, traces of a stone circle 30 feet in diameter.

Two of the ancient pillars now in West Park, Macclesfield

Cluelow or Clulow Cross... the pillar is now hidden by trees but the man-made mound is easily seen.

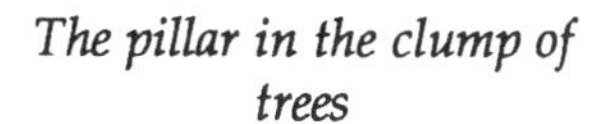

The pillar in the clump of trees

A close-up of the top of the pillar. Compare it with those at West Park, Macclesfield and at Leek Churchyard.

The nearby stone circle as seen in the late 1800s

Flint arrow head and knife from stone circle Clulow Cross.

The stone circle as it is today

Standingstone

At the crossroads above Forest Chapel. There is a memorial plaque to the late Walter Smith by the roadside.

At the top of the lane that skirts Trentabank Reservoir, there is an area known as Standingstone. At this spot the road is joined by one coming from the bottom of Oven Lane or, by another route, from Forest Chapel over Rainslow. The lane then descends to the Clough Road in the valley opposite the entrance to Dry Knowl. On certain older ordnance survey maps is marked "Site of Cross".

Where is it now? I would imagine it is forming one side of a gatepost or perhaps it is part of a drystone wall. It was certainly in situ in the year 1810 for it is described by the Rev. W Marriott in his work "Antiquities of Lyme".

The Reverend Gentleman was a trifle long-winded. After lengthily describing the beauty of the area, he says ". . . the attention is unexpectedly drawn to a solitary unostentatious object of stone . . . it is composed of a flat base deposited on the ground with a prominency of pillar rising from its plan". In other words, a Standing Stone.

He continues: "The figure of the base is a parrallelogram or oblong containing in its centre a square socket; from which springs a tall slender pillar once placed in equilibrio, and squared in its horizontal circumference. Time, however, by its weight, has given to the upright a declination of about two inches; whilst the weather has somewhat rounded its angles at the top, and the points of the parrallegram likewise in the base of the southern side. From the same cause, the pillar has received a slope downward of a taperlike form excepting that its largest bulk is in the middle; and the native pores of the stone have been enlarged into crevices on the north-eastern corner. "The conformation is summed up in these particulars; being totally devoid of every extraneous ornament, such as a carving or inscription:

Base	*feet*	*inches*
Length	3	0
Breadth	2	0
Depth above ground		6
Pillar		
Height	4	0
Breadth in middle		10
Breadth at top		4

And then, after this long-winded explanation, the Reverend Gentleman at last gets to the point of it all. He says, in conclusion: "It was the site of the burial of suicides".

Crossroads were important places. They were looked upon in Celtic and pre-Celtic times as the meeting and parting of the ways. They were places where the supernatural occurred. They were places where witches were murdered so their souls did not know which way to go. They were the places criminals were hanged. Suicides were buried at or near crossroads and an early nineteenth century map shows "burial place" by Standing Stone.

Crossroads have been referred to as the haunt of the devil. They were also considered to be places where cures could be carried out. Standing stones often had enough earth power to affect certain cures and the two together at the Forest crossroads must have been dramatically effective to the believers.

Hanging Stone – Swythamley

Along the Congleton to Buxton road (A54) turn right at the Rose and Crown, signposted Gradbach. Park at the Gradbach public car park. Follow the path marked Swythamley then the path for Hanging Stone Farm. Alternatively, take the footpath around the Swythamley Estate for Hanging Stone Farm.

An awesome and menacing rock structure called Hanging Stone lurks about one mile away from Lud Church, a magical and mystical crevice which we shall explore later.

It's difficult to imagine that this could have been designed by Mother Nature. The projecting rocks, two of which are flat and laid table-wise upon the brow of a precipice overlooking Swythamley Park are something of an enigma.

It is believed that hangings once took place at the Hanging Stone, but it must be said that evidence of human or indeed animal sacrifice is scarce. In the early 1800s, it was recorded in the Gentleman's Magazine, that local superstitions in the high moorlands alleged the rock was the scene of sacrifices and, said the article, the structure was held in awe by the locals, who told of the site being the place where sacrifices were made to the Earth Mother.

Earlier, in 1708, the then vicar of Leek and a noted historian, the Reverend Thomas Loxdale discussed the shape of the rock and surmised it was certainly man-made. He thought the artificial structure was a hill altar or devotion stone on which sacrifices had been offered.

Certainly, these rocks can tell a tale or two. In the year 1834, a forester by the name of Hughes was working on the Swythamley Estate and digging holes ready to plant new trees at the base of Hanging Stone, and discovered gold, silver and copper coins. One was a Cannon Mint, made from melted down cannons and others were from the time of the Civil War. There was also a gold coin "of much earlier date".

Examination of Hanging Stone does show that there is a definite symmetry about the rocks. The Reverend Gentleman who inspected the site, remarked on this in addition to his sacrifice theory. He wrote ". . . the bulk, shape and position (of the rocks) are exactly the same; the levels and squares the same; all of which, in my opinion bespeak a design, such regularity being rarely seen in works of chance."

The Hanging Stone, on which there are two plaques. The first, dedicated to Courtney Brocklehurst by his brother reads: "Lt.Col. Henry Courtney Brocklehurst, 10th Royal Hussars and pilot in the Royal Flying Corps 1916-1918. Game Warden of the Sudan. Born at Swythamley May 27th 1888, killed on active service in Burma on Commando June 1942. Horses he loved and laughter, the sun, wide spaces and the open air. The trust of all dumb living things he won and never knew the luck too good to share. His were the simple heart and the open hand and honest faults he never strove to hide. Problems of life he could not understand but as a man would wish to die he died. Now, though he will not ride with us again, his merry spirit seems our comfort yet. Freed from the power of memories and pain, forbidding us to mourn or to forget. Erected by his devoted brother, 1949". The second one reads: "Beneath this rock August 1st 1874 was buried Burke, a noble mastiff, black and tan. Faithful as woman, braver than man. A gun and a ramble his heart's desire with a friend of his life, the Swythamley Squire".

Throughout this book I have endeavoured to lay emphasis on the need to honour people's private property. There is a clearly defined pathway to the Hanging Stone, for instance.

Courtney Brocklehurst

The Squire of Swythamley buried his favourite hunting mastiff below the rocks in 1871. The dog's name was Burke, (its companion had been Hare).

In the late 1950s a tablet was placed on the stone in memory of Lt. Col. Courtney Brocklehurst, 10th Royal Hussars. This devil-may-care member of the Brocklehurst dynasty was killed while swimming across a river in Burma in 1942. He was on a spying mission, it was disclosed much later.

Before the Second World War, he was a familiar and dashing figure around the villages of the high moorland. My own father recalled him driving up to the Three Horse Shoes Inn at Meerbrook, (now called the Lazy Trout), at the wheel of a vintage Bentley – before James Bond was placed in a similar vehicle. The "Young Squire" bought drinks for everyone in the pub and swapped stories with them concerning the game thereabouts. He was fully aware they all poached on his land, but they were mostly tenants of his family, and they kept an eye out for anything untoward.

Locals could indeed, take titbits from the land, but a stranger would find himself looking down the barrels of a shotgun.

Courtney had been to the Antarctic which his elder brother Philip and Shackleton in the ship, The Nimrod. The Ship Inn at Wincle was so named because a picture of the Nimrod hung there, the story goes, but in fact it was so named because a Liverpool ship owner called one of his vessels The Swythamley. Sailors nicknamed it the Sweet Emily and it was wrecked on the Blenheim Reef, near the Cape.

The figurehead was a sportsman with two dogs representing the Swythamley Squire, Sir Philip, with his favourite hounds, Burke and Hare.

Courtney, the dashing army officer had been at one point in his romantic life, a game warden in the Sudan, and his fondness for animals was reflected in the fact that he kept a private zoo at his home. This zoo was swelled early in the Second World War, when animals from Whipsnade Zoo were brought north to the Swythamley Estate, to escape the German bombs.

During a fire, many of the animals escaped and included among them were some wallabies. Most of the other animals were recaptured except these, and a couple of llamas. The larger animals died but the marsupials survived and can sometimes be seen to this day, although very rarely. Several locals are fully aware of where these animals hide out, but a visitor in search of them will never be told the location.

Swythamley Park, when it was the residence of Sir P.L. Brocklehurst, Bart

Jenkin Chapel – Saltersford, Rainow

Turn right off the A5002 Macclesfield-Whaley Bridge road, half a mile after passing through Rainow. Bear left at Blue Boar farm.

For over 250 years, the tiny chapel of Saltersford, near Rainow, commonly known as Jenkin Chapel but officially named the Church of St John the Baptist has stood proudly and firmly holding out against the worst of what the high moorland weather can throw at it.

As its name implies, Saltersford was the ford of the Salters – packmen who drove their horses, mules and carts across the ancient salt trails from the Cheshire salt pans to Yorkshire. Jenkin Chapel was built in 1733 by farmers and at first it resembled a farmhouse, for only later was a tower added. Jenkin was, it is understood, a drover who used the ancient way of the salt jaggers (the early transporters of cargoes along the trackways) some 300 years ago, driving sheep and cattle betwixt North Wales and the Peak District. This man was also a religious soul and something of a preacher, for he attracted people from localities where he would rest for the night and hold forth on the righteousness of the Lord's word.

A preaching cross was built by the crossroads where Jenkin Chapel now stands and there our Jenkin the Drover would preach. This sight proved to be the natural gathering place for religious ceremonies after Jenkin passed on and the church was built, to be known as the Church at Jenkin's Cross and later curtailed to Jenkin Chapel. It is also referred to as Jenkin's Chapel on some maps in some reference books.

Only a short way up the road from the Chapel, in Eurin Lane, is a memorial to John Turner, a user of the trackway who perished in the snow during a winter's night in or about the year 1735. The inscription tells of the mystery of a lone footprint in the snow by the side of the body. At the top of the lane is the Blue Boar Farm where once stood a revered stone, the Blue Boar Stone or Cross. In the name "Eurin" we have, said the late Walter Smith, a short form of what might originally have been the old English Eoforwine, meaning Boar Friend or Boar Protector. Today we would call such a person a gamekeeper.

The stone on Eurin Lane carries the inscription: "Here John Turner was cast away in a heavy snow storm in the night in or about the year 1733. The print of a woman's shoe was found by his side, in the snow where he lay dead".

Jenkin or Jenkin's Chapel

The memorial stone to John Turner, who died in a snowstorm. The other side refers to the strange story of the footprint.

Bearing the Rushes

From Langley to the Leathers Smithy pub, take the left fork for about a mile.

At Forest Chapel, the tiny church in Macclesfield Forest which has the official name of St Stephen's, the annual Rushbearing Service takes place on a Sunday afternoon in the middle of August. Each year crowds flock to the quaint place of worship to witness the ceremony.

Thomas Newton of Butley near Macclesfield refers to the custom in a book "Herbal of the Bible" dated 1589 and says: "With sedges and rushes many in the county do use in summer time to strew their parlours and churches as well as for coolness as for pleasant smell". The custom is observed at some churches in the Lake District, especially at Ambleside and Grasmere. The rushes borne in procession at these places are shaped into some ambitious designs including standards of giant rushes, harps, rushes, moss, evergreens and flowers.

In "Rushbearing" by Alfred Burton in 1901 the custom is said to have been observed in a former period at Wincle as well. No-one I have spoken to has heard tell of rushbearing at Wincle Church, so I would surmise it was over a century ago. A passage in his book says: *"At Forest Chapel near Macclesfield, the little church is usually crowded on Rushbearing Sunday. Until a comparatively recent time the floor of Wincle Church was neither paved nor flagged, but spread with rushes. These were removed annually on a certain Sunday in July when it was customary to decorate a cart with flowers and bear them to church. This was celebrated with great rejoicing and was termed the 'rush bearing' and in after years when rushes were no longer used, the drinking and the name were still kept up but they are wisely discontinued".*

At the Forest Chapel, nothing very elaborate is done with the rushes, only a little decorations and the simple expedient of strewing the floor of the Chapel and the approach is resorted to. When the annual service began at the Chapel in the Forest, is not known; the first mention of it in the church accounts is in 1848. Something very strange and unlooked for happened at that Rushbearing. What it was nobody knows, but after it was all over, a sum of five shillings was paid "To William Smith for Repairing the windows at the Chapel and School, broken at the Memorable Rush Bearing".

This is the first recorded Rushbearing and it certainly was memorable, but the tantalising reference gives us no more clues.

This was taken around the turn of the century at the Forest in the Chapel. Rushes can be seen at the church entrance and the crowds are "overspill" from the ceremony. Picture loaned by Mrs Lea of Macclesfield.

The Rushbearing ceremony as it is today during the middle of August. If you want to witness it, be sure to be there early. Perhaps a picnic lunch wouldn't be too bad an idea beforehand, to take advantage of the beauty of the area.

The Rushbearing is an event looked forward to with great interest by the parishioners and by their friends, not to mention hikers, cyclists and motorists who journey to the novel ceremony.

The Churchyard of Forest Chapel contains a few tombstones of interest. On one of these is recorded the death of a Forest farmer named George Goodwin of Longclough. Longclough is just to the left of the great bend in Buxton Road beneath Shining Tor. It is said that Goodwin who lived to be over 100 could repeat, without book, any passage of scripture and that he retained all his faculties until his death.

"Here lie the remains of Ann, wife of George Goodwin, of Long Clough, Macclesfield Forest, who departed this life, January 14 1781, aged 86 years. Remember now thy Creator in the days of thy youth, while the evil days come not, nor the Years draw nigh, when though shalt say, I have no pleasure in them. Also the above said George Goodwin, who departed this life, October 1783, aged 105."

On the opposite side of our Land of the Three Shires – at Ipstones, south of Leek, there is a gravestone which records William Beresford of Park Head who died in 1704 aged 116. But there is one to beat that, for I have come across a record of Mary Brookes of Horton, near Rudyard, who died January 5th 1787, aged 119 years. Thus the females carry off the palm for long life.

Wincle Church – Rushbearing ceremonies were once held there as well as at Forest Chapel.

Lud Church – Back Forest

From Gradbach Youth Hostel, take the footpath along the Dane then follow signs to Swythamley. Fork left when you see a stone sign marked 'Lud Church'.

The Green Chapel of Sir Gawain – or the Church of the Sun God?

In the wooded area known as Back Forest, about one mile and a quarter north from Swythamley Hall there is a curious chasm known as Lud Church or Lud's Church. Its significance to Celts and the followers of the Old Religion, not to mention the 15th Century Lollards is, or was, immense.

A worthy writer earlier this century, Mr. Walter Smith, says of Lud Church: "On a sloping hillside of Swythamley, between the High Forest and the Dane, a ravine called Ludchurch is a traditional place of meeting of worshippers in the olden time. But no registers, no tombstones, no tablet can tell the tale."

A description in the year 1683 says: "A narrow but well beaten path conducted me through a forest which, in some places, was so extremely dense, that all the view of the sky was precluded. The forest appeared to be several miles in extent and abounded in fine ancient trees...at a length I reached the mouth of a gloomy looking glen into which I entered. The place was extremely narrow with damp walls rising to a considerable height. The top was so overgrown with heather, that little light could penetrate the place; consequently a deep gloom pervaded."

Ludchurch is a rent running through millstone grit for about 100 yards from 30 to 40 feet in depth and from 6 to 10 feet wide. The sides are vertical and overhanging, and a flight of twenty-four steps leads out of the place at its southern end, but the ravine itself winds on for a few yards further until it terminates in a deep hole. From the bottom of this hole, the renowned cavern of Ludchurch descends far below the roof, in places being a great height. Explorers have thought they have heard a great noise, possibly the River Dane.

In the 1870s, a local resident, William Mills, armed with a rope a lantern and a large ball of twine went underground for some hours and "thought that there were some signs of Druidical remains", and also steps having the appearance of masonry.

In a book dated 1682 called "Natural History of Staffordshire", it is reported that the sides are so steeped and hanging over that it sometimes preserves snow all summer. A Quarnford man brought a sack of snow to Leek Fair on July 17th and poured it down at the mercat (market) cross saying he could fetch a hundred load of it.

One legend abounds of Lud Church, and this also purports to be the reason the place got its name. I hope to prove otherwise to you.

The story is said to have been told to Sir William de Lacy who visited the district in the reign of Henry VIII, and is concerned with the shooting of Alice de Lud Auk by the military while they were breaking up a meeting of worshippers about the year 1405.

The legend is as follows: "At some time in the Middle Ages a small band of Lollards made this ravine a place of retreat. Their leader was an old man named Walter de Lud-Auk and his followers were called Luddites. Soldiers had searched for them without success till their singing betrayed their hiding place. This was guarded at the entrance by Henril Montair, the forester of the estate, who attempted to prevent the soldiers from entering. During the struggle a shot was fired into the ravine killing the beautiful granddaughter of the aged leader. Her body was solemnly buried near the entrance and then the party surrendered and were taken to France. It is said that Montair escaped to France but that Lud-Auk died in confinement. Hence, we are told, Lud Church was named after Walter de Lud-Auk.

This is wrong. The aged follower of John Wycliffe, the founder of the Lollards, is in fact named after Lud Church and not the other way around! The name Walter de Lud-Auk simply means Walter of Lud Church (*Auk* is an Old English form of word meaning temple or church).

Lud or *Llud* or possibly *Nudd* was a Celtic sky god. The Celts worshipped this deity throughout their lands. There was a temple to Llud at the site of St Paul's Cathedral in London. It was later called by the Saxons *Ludes Geat* and is now known as Ludgate. Lud's wife was called Anu, Annu or Dana and a prominent Celtic tribe was the Tuatha de Danaans or "folk of the god whose mother is Dana".

The "mother" of the area around Lud's Church is undoubtedly the River Dane. It is easy to see where the River Dane derives its name. Think too of Danes Moss immediately to the south of Macclesfield, also stemming from Dana the Earth Mother.

Dana was the Celt's Earth Mother. Her son, Lud was worshipped at Lud's Temple or Church at that Sacred Grove in the Forest.

Taking the Celtic aspect just a little further (I could go much deeper but feel the point is made) more proof of the Celts in the area comes from the name Lamaload, now a water board reservoir in the Macclesfield Forest area. August 1st was Lhuany's Day, which name refers to the god Lugh who was remembered annually in the fire festival on August 1st. The festival was called Lugnasad. The Christianised name for the day is Lammas.

The awesome Lud or Lud's Church cavern

An old photograph of the bridge over the River Dane. Was the river named after a Celtic goddess?

In search of the Green Knight

The area of Lud Church, the Roaches and Macclesfield Forest could possibly be the setting of a mediaeval poem of Sir Gawain and the Green Knight but others prefer the Wirral as the likely area.

However, R.W.V. Elliott firmly believes it was the land between Macclesfield Leek, Axe Edge and The Roaches where Sir Gawain pursued the Green Knight in the poem before coming to the Green Chapel (Lud Church).

Also mentioned in the poem is the manor house or castle and I think this refers to Swythamley.

Strange race of beings

"Legends of the Moorland and Forest in North Staffordshire" written by a Miss Dakeyne in 1860 says: "Until a few years ago the subterranean cavern which issues from Lud Church was inhabited by a strange and distinct race of beings".

Unfortunately she goes no further but tantilisingly refers to "a loud crowing" emitting from the cavern.

In Old English, the word "Hlud" means "The Loud One". It is pronounced "Lud".

Miss Dakeyne also tells us: "Some years ago an eccentric artist in one of his excursions to Lud Church resolved to take a hawk's nest which he saw high up on the rocks; and with the aid of a ladder he succeeded, at the risk of his life. One of his best young friends, still more daring, caused himself to be let down by a rope through the opening above and accomplished in safety his hazardous and dangerous purpose, the birds hovering around him and uttering the most piercing cries.

More tellingly, Miss Dakeyne says a student once explored the cavern. He left a newspaper and coins as tokens of his visit and as he returned "a terrible clap, as of thunder, seemed to threaten the closing of the small aperture by which they had entered".

I refer you again to the name meaning "The Loud One".

Lucky Charms

Four miles north of Leek, standing as a backdrop to Ludchurch, are the ragged outcrops known as The Roaches.

A number of dolmens or ancient burial sites have been found on them and at one time evidence of the reverence the area held was shown by reason of the fact that amulets made from stone carved from these rocks were sold as charms to be worn around the neck.

An amulet or lucky charm made from stone from the Roaches

Cannibals of Caster's Bridge

From Gradbach Youth Hostel along the River Dane

Caster's Bridge went over Black Brook – a stream named from the colour of the soil or pebbles over which it runs – and which joins the River Dane twenty yards below the bridge.

The tale is told of a traveller along the Forest road – a road not then taken by travellers if it could be avoided. If any needed to take that road through the Forest they travelled in bands armed with staves, it was said.

As night fell, the traveller espied a lonely cottage near the river side with a mastiff standing by the door. A man wearing a grisly beard came to the door and close behind a woman stood. They asked the stranger in. he asked if he could stay the night and settled down to his bed, calling for his supper.

He heard "the slow and distant tread of many feet" and thought the family must be busy melting ore for there was a great light and heat coming from an oven. He went to the door and opened the latch a little more and heard a child say: "Mother, when will that queer old man be dead? I'm sure the oven will soon be very hot".

The Traveller made a quick getaway down the river and climbed up the riverbank at Caster's bridge whereupon he realised he was being chased by women, men and dogs.

Eventually he made good his escape and went to the nearest town, presumably Leek, from where the local militia rode out and dragged the wretched inmates from that infested place and burned their home to the ground.

There is a tradition that gold has from time to time been found where these ruins once lay.

Caster's Bridge – its name was originally Smelter's or Melter's Bridge.
Photo: C. Rathbone

Around the Roaches, coal and metals were mined; the rock had magical qualities and was worn as amulets. Many men who lived in the Quarnford area had to find employment other than in the local quarries and coalmines. This group, early this century, were employed at Tatton's Dyeworks, Upperhulme, and includes members of the Pickfords from the Quarnford area. They were rugged chaps, they had to be to survive the hard winters that nature threw at them.

The road to the Roaches, beyond which lay Flash and then Buxton. The main road from Leek pictured about 1902.

Dolmen near Rock Hall, Roaches

Dolmen, Roaches

A picnic party on The Roaches at the beginning of the 20th century. Photo:E. Oldham

Flash, where the road goes off to Royal Cottage and Leek.

Squatter's Rights at Quarnford

About six miles out of Leek, on the Buxton (A53) road, turn sharp left – signposted "Flash", also for the New Inn.

Close by Three Shire Heads is the tiny hamlet of Flash, in the village of Quarnford. In my book, "A Portait of Macclesfield", I mention the Flash coiners, those rogues who made counterfeit "Flash Money", and used the expedient of being able to cross the Three Shires of Cheshire, Derbyshire and Staffordshire to avoid capture.

Some believe the Flashmen were much maligned and that the transgressors were not natives of Flash but the travelling badgers and hawkers who had settled in an around the place because the desolate countryside suited their purposes well.

As it happens, my own family come from the area now known as Flash in the Parish of Quarnford and so their innocence I am happy to account for. The Pickford family occupied many farmsteads and buildings around the Quarnford area, working the open cast coal mines and the quarries. The family tree has been traced back to the early 1700s and a legend within the family is that the Pickfords arrived and established Squatters' Rights by building a house within a day. Legality was apparently established if smoke could be seen from the chimney within that day. The story within the family goes that this most certainly took place at Ferny Knowle, which is still a residence but not now, I hasten to add, anything to do with those "Squatters' Rights".

Flash is also famous for being the highest village in England. It is 1518 feet above sea level and it also has the distinction of being the most northerly point of Staffordshire. The village consists of a church, a school, a pub, post office and a few houses, plus a village hall. The church was built in 1744 and rebuilt in 1901. Electricity only came to the village in 1962 and it was 1984 before the properties were connected to mains water.

In early June, the village celebrates its annual feast day which is called the Tea Pot Parade. This celebrates the formation of the Tea Pot Club which derived its name from the practice of keeping money in a tea pot. In those far off days, before the National Health Service, people would keep their spare halfpennies and farthings in teapots, to be used when illness struck, or in case a burial had to be paid for. The people of Flash

Isaac and Mary Pickford, great, great grandparents of the author. The Pickford family were residents of Quarnford for centuries and many were buried at Flash Church.

and Quarnford formed a Friendly Society, with the idea that regular collections were made by an elected Committee and all proceeds kept in the tea pot. Whenever a family needed to use the monetary contents of the teapot, a committee member would call and empty the entire money onto the kitchen table. The collection would then start again until the next person or persons needed to have the contents emptied.

This has been going for at least 200 years and the Tea Pot Club is still going strong, although no longer is a teapot used. Nowadays, the subscriptions are paid into the bank, but death and sickness benefits are still given out.

Today the celebration takes the form of a procession from the village hall to the Travellers Rest across the main Leek to Buxton Road at Flash Bar – the site of the former toll bar on the turnpike road. It formerly commenced at the Methodist Chapel in the village but this has now become a private residence.

In 1991, I had the pleasure of speaking to Mr Horace Poole, the Chairman of the Flash Loyal Union Society, to give the Teapot Club its more official, but not as appealing title. He spoke to me about the bleak winters that Flash and the surrounding areas still "enjoy" and told me the story of how, when his brother died during the Second World War at the farm they were in at Flash, the snow and ice delayed burial for several months. And even then, the funeral party had to walk to the burial because of the bad weather. Perhaps it is now not surprising that Mr Poole was living in the relative comfort of Macclesfield when I spoke to him. The Club, said Mr Poole, was once referred to by Mr John Sales, J.P. Chairman of Leek Magistrates, for many years, as being run by "The best men in England". Never once had there been a halfpenny missing from the Club's accounts.

How different from the Flash men of old, whether they had been those tinkers and scoundrels or actually men of Flash. Certainly the men who ran and still run the Tea Pot Club, were and still are men of complete honesty and integrity.

Flash Loyal Union Society (the Tea Pot Club) in the late 1800s.

On the steps of the Methodist Church, Mr Horace Poole, later to become the Chairman of the Flash Loyal Union Society, or the Tea Pot Club. The procession is just about to leave during the celebrations round about the year 1940.

The Tea Pot Club parade round about 1950. Picture: Horace Poole.

Flash Infants School perform the ancient Maypole ceremony (see the section on Rushton customs). This photograph, again by Mr Horace Poole, was taken about 1954 and shows his twin daugters, Jessica and Margaret Poole then aged about seven years, with other pupils.

Defeating the Dragon

As Abbott Mellitus prepared to leave for the British Isles in June of the year 601 AD Pope Gregory wrote to him: "I have come to the conclusion that the temples of the idols in England should not on any account be destroyed. Augustine must smash the idols but the temples themselves should be sprinkled with holy water and altars set up in them in which relics are to be enclosed . . ."I hope the people (seeing their temples are not destroyed) will leave their idolatry and yet continue to frequent the places as formerly, so coming to know and revere the true God".

The folklore concerning St George and St Michael slaying the dragon is seen as the new religion conquering the sold. The dragon, serpent or sometimes the worm, is the old religion.

Many pre-Christian sites were on hills for a number of reasons. One was because of the earth energy emanating and another, as at Leek, was because of what could be witnessed as well.

The majority of churches that can claim to have taken over from the pagan gods are, therefore, on raised sites and are usually dedicated to St Michael or St George.

The Parish Church of St Michael and All Angels at Macclesfield most certainly was founded on a site venerated by pre-Christians. At the east end of the Church within the sanctuary there are two pieces of stone with, it is said, Saxon markings and bits of a Saxon cross.

This church was formerly called All Saints or All Hallows and did not become St Michaels until 1739. But why did it then become St Michaels? I think the truth is it reverted to its old name in that year.

And at Leek the ancient church now dedicated to St Edward the Confessor would have been dedicated to another Saint prior to his ascendency.

Which one? A clue is in the fact that adjacent to the Church is the town's oldest inn, now called the Swan.

Previously it was the Green Dragon.

And what could be seen from the hill where the church was sited? Certainly in Leek's case the answer is simple. Every year on the Midsummer Solstice the sun can be seen to set behind Bosley Cloud and then re-appear only to set again.

The double sunset still attracts crowds every year but unfortunately the night has to be cloudless and the last time the double sunset was witnessed in its entirety from the viewing point at the back of the church was in 1958! To compound the problem, trees are now beginning to block the view as well.

It is possible to see the double sunset from other areas around Leek, notably on the Roaches, but this site is the pure one.

Both country and townsfolk were far more superstitious in days past than now. The slightest thing out of the ordinary could hold fear. A shadow, a natural phenomena previously unexperienced or,as in this case, an innocent piece of wood. This Dragon was discovered near to Back Forest on the Roaches in Autumn 1991.

Macclesfield's Church of St Michael and All Angels, as it was in the late nineteenth century. Old stones show it was a religious site before Christianity came to these shores.

Macclesfield's Church on the hill, now dedicated to St Michael. The town's famous 108 steps are shown in this 1920s picture.

The Parish Church of St Edward the Confessor at Leek – the site of the viewing of the double sunset

Prestbury's Dragon

Prestbury's Church is built 22 and a half degrees out of true orientation, said the late Mr Raymond Richards of Gawsworth Hall in his fine book "Old Cheshire Churches".

This may be unusual but the answer is simple to any dowser or person who has heard of ley lines, earth lines or call them what you will. They used to be called dragon lines, and the Church is sited on one.

The original Christian church at Prestbury was probably laid to waste by the Normans before they re-built and now, in a glass case outside the church are fragments of two ancient cross shafts. Look closely at these and it is easy to determine the outline of a dragon.

Above: Prestbury Church, where a Saxon Cross clearly shows a carving of a dragon – Good overcoming Evil [the Pagan Church]. It can be found in a glass case in the churchyard. Below, the Norman Chapel:

Black and White Witches

The subject of witchcraft nowadays seems only to rear its head in those old Hammer horror films and some Sunday newspapers.

Yet not so very long ago, the town of Leek was riddled with superstition concerning the creatures of darkness.

And so was its neighbour, Macclesfield.

Both towns had ducking stools where a person convicted of witchcraft could be punished and in both towns it was also a way of discovering if the accused was guilty or not.

All too often an elderly person was the subject of this torture in the seventeenth and even eighteenth centuries and the act caused much merriment among spectators. Perhaps there is a parallel with the French Revolution and the spectators at the guillotine.

The hills between Macclesfield and Leek have many a tale to tell if they could but speak. Preachers used to wander these hills of Macclesfield Forest, Wincle, Quarnford and the 'Clough and be invited to cast out devils. These devils may have been inhabiting the farmer's cattle or swine, they thought.

A group of these preachers had a church at Meerbrook. One such preacher was Hugh Bourne who came from Tunstall and won many souls to Christ by his way of talking. Another was James Nixon who used to wear out the knees of his trousers praying in Leek Market Place.

Once, Nixon was on his knees in the Market Place and townsfolk threw fruit and vegetables at him. He carried on. They then turned on a water engine and pumped water over him and still he prayed.

An elderly woman, conversant with the black arts, was named Jennie Roberts and she lived in the middle of the nineteenth century. She exercised all her powers on a farmer who lived near Quarnford. But, finding she was unable to do grievous bodily harm on account of the farmer and his wife carrying a good supply of witch elm she turned her art on their cattle, with fatal results. The cows would not give their usual supply of milk, the pigs pined away, and the calves went mad and ultimately died; nor could a white witch be found in the neighbourhood with sufficient power to remove the direful spell.

The farmer and his wife had to remove from the neighbourhood to Swythamley where they lived in peace.

An old lady who lived in the Watercoates, Macclesfield, practised the witch's arts but was not so bad as she had been represented. A contributor to a local paper of over 100 years ago had this to say about her:

> *"She was often a visitor at my mother's house when I was a boy and she took great pains to warn me against Black Witches and to instruct me in the art of a White Witch. I have sat for hours in her cottage watching her bake oatcakes and listening to her stories about Black Witches. She always had a small tub, or what she more often called a 'dashun' of salt by the fire from which she threw a handful into the fire when anyone passed and looked into her cottage whom she did not like or whom she suspected of witchcraft".*

Urban Blackmail

It was not only the country folk who lived in fear of these dark souls. It was also the silk workers.

An old document in my possession tells of a person who lived in Kiln Lane, Leek, in the 1870s who operated a form of "protection racket". She was well known to the townsfolk and they believed she had the craft of a witch. She was a terror to the bobbin turners who occupied a workshop adjoining what is now the Brindley Mill Museum in Mill Street.

She was supposed to practise her art by loosening the iron wheels in the workshop but more often than not she would throw the straps off the machines, preventing the operatives from working. The owner had to send a message to her telling her she could have a drink at a nearby ale house. This was an invitation she never refused and after she had drunk her fill the workers could return and they would find – time and again, it is said – that both wheels and straps were working all right.

A White Witch employed her art for healing purposes. A Black Witch would exercise her art on anyone who offended her, or for reward.

A Castle's Protection

A castellated mansion, commonly called Macclesfield Castle once stood majestically at the top of Mill Street (see my book *A Portrait of Macclesfield*).

But as grand as this structure was, it needed the help of the supernatural to keep it safe.

Above the entrance to the stately building there was a figure assumed to have been placed there to ward away the evil eye.

Its description is thus: It was set at such a height that it could not be seen from below; it was Asiatic or Egyptian in appearance; it had a low and much receeding forehead; it had long hair combed back straight and broad down its back; its body was slim and rather feminine; its clenched hands were fixed to its sides and it had long feet.

It does not take much imagination to see it was a caricature of an elf or fairy.

Ghostly Goings On

Certain areas of towns and villages have an unpleasant reputation, either rightly or wrongly. One part of Macclesfield for instance was recorded as being the abode of a number of elderly ladies who dabbled in the black arts. It was the part of town around the corner of Buxton Road and Davenport Street of which a writer to the Macclesfield Times in the early part of the century said: "Almost 75 years ago, certain people lived in cottages there who would have been ducked in the town's Ducking Stool, had it still been in existence."

The Ducking Stool was used at Cuckstoolpit Hill, close by the area we are referring to, strangely enough. This photograph shows the Royal Oak Hotel which was at the corner of Buxton Road and Davenport Street and a party of "regulars" who were, no doubt, preparing for an outing, just about the time of the First World War. In the early part of this century, there was a murder in one of the cottages just along Davenport Street from where the Royal Oak was situated. A young woman was killed by a local man, Ernest Thornley, who was found guilty of the crime and hanged at Knutsford Jail. The house was no more than 75 yards from the pub, which during the beginning of the 1990s became a car fitting establishment and the local newspaper, the Macclesfield Express, carried a story on its front page about the workers there hearing strange noises and seeing some ghostly apparitions.

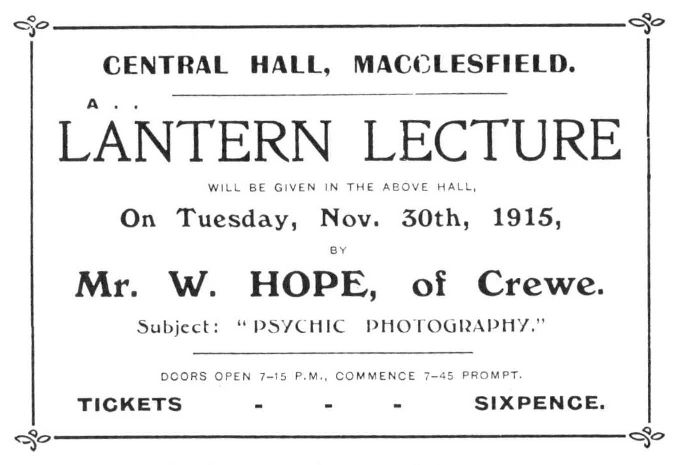

Investigations into the unexplained in 1915.

The last licensee of the public house, before it closed and became Gleave Motors and later Kwik Fit, was a man named Ossie Dearden, the son of a very well known Manchester businessman.

Regulars at "The Royal Oak" – a site said to be haunted.

Maggoty's Ghost – at Gawsworth

Gawsworth is on the A536 Macclesfield to Congleton road; follow the signs for Gawsworth Hall

It is said that the ghost of a court jester haunts a wood at Gawsworth. Maggoty Johnson's Wood is named after the character whose real name was Samuel Johnson. The appendage "Maggoty" has nothing to do with the decaying state of the poor man, but was a Cheshire dialect expression for someone "not quite right in the head."

Many stories are related of Johnson, a local character of eccentric habit. He was also known as "Lord Flame" and would seem to have been a Jack of all trades, for with the profession of a dancing master, he united that of a wit, poet, musician and an actor. "Hurlothrumbo" was his chief production and it had a run of thirty successive nights at The Haymarket, London, in 1729. This man was also an entertainer in the royal courts, a latter-day court jester. An amusing tale is told of Johnson being relegated to the village stocks, while in the state of inebriety, by some actor visitors to Gawsworth. This seems to have had such a profound effect upon him that writing to a friend in London at the time, he says he "will have to make a retreat from his beloved Gawsworth and leave no trace behind."

Johnson was presented in his old age with a small house in the village by the Earl of Harrington and on his deathbed he requested that his body should not be buried in the churchyard, but in the wood where it now lies.

An idyllic day in the 1930s at Maggoty Johnson's grave. Hikers read the inscription and an elderly gent lights his pipe. There is a tradition that if you walk round his grave a certain number of times, he will come to life.

The Dark Lady

Much has been written concerning the Dark Lady of Shakespeare's Sonnets and much has also been written with the assumption that she was none other than Mistress Mary Fitton of the village of Gawsworth. Her ghost is supposed to walk at Gawsworth Hall, that delightful black and white structure which attracts visitors from all over the globe, and it is also supposed to walk at Gawsworth Churchyard. A third claim to her spirit is Gawsworth Rectory and she is even supposed to walk down the lane from the Harrington Arms, a busy lady indeed.

Some twenty or so years ago, a special church court was held when certain people wanted to investigate whether her remains were under the floor of the church. This was not allowed and so Mary can still rest in relative peace.

Mary, a beautiful lady by any standards, was an attendant at the court of Queen Elizabeth and she is supposed to have caught the eye of the Bard of Avon.

At Gawsworth Hall, it is told that the smell of incense can sometimes be experienced, emanating from a bedroom immediately under the Priest's Room. There is much to be investigated at Gawsworth and perhaps the years may divulge some more secrets, about Mary and the other wandering Gawsworth spirit, Maggoty Johnson.

Gawsworth Church and Lake

Leek's Roebuck Inn

Leek's picturesque black and white Roebuck Inn on Derby Street has been an architectural feature of the town since 1626 when its framework was brought in detached pieces from Shropshire. It was first opened as The Sun but on a date not known, the name was changed to that of the Roebuck. All its local life it has been a leading hostelry and was used as a coaching inn in the old days for the four-in-hands travelling between Manchester and London and Birmingham and Manchester. For many years it was owned by the Lowndes family and when they put it up for sale in 1876, it was bought by a Mrs Byrom for £4,120, later being taken over – in 1882 – by Messrs Bell and Co of Burton.

The Roebuck. Like many hostelries, it has been said it is haunted. The Bulls Head in Macclesfield Market Place has a room – number 13 – where the apparition of a woman has been seen floating through the wall.

Bosley Cloud and Bully Thrumble

Take the A523 Macclesfield to Leek road. Pass the Crown and Fox Inns. At the crossroads, a clearly-marked path and steps lead to The Cloud.

The construction of the Macclesfield canal vastly altered the shape of towering Bosley Cloud, that magnificent outcrop where ancient man once built fortresses and churches.

"Navvies" used stone from the Cloud to build the "Cut" and later it supplied stone for the foundations of the magnificent viaduct at North Rode when the railways came along. Prior to this official vandalism it had four curious points jutting out of that part of the Cloud that stands in the parish of Rushton Spencer. These were known as Sugar Rock, Raven Rock, Mareback and Bully Thrumble. The Bully Thrumble looked like a natural corkscrew and rose 60 or 70 feet above the Cloud. It must have been quite a sight.

It is hardly surprising our ancestors looked upon the Cloud as something rather special. From it can be seen Leek, Macclesfield, Congleton, Shutlinslow, Mow Cop, Gun Ridge and the Roaches and, on a clear day, the Welsh mountains.

Close to the Congleton road is Drummers Knob and this part of the Cloud is often used by picnickers. Locals say it is haunted by the ghost of a drummer boy from Bonny Prince Charlie's army who was shot when he stopped to rest as the Prince's soldiers travelled from Macclesfield to Leek. This explains, they say, why people who stop at the grassy area almost invariably pack up their picnics and leave before they have finished. However, a farmer explained that the land is unobstructed on every side and, while commanding lovely views is also very exposed to the elements – in other words; it gets very cold there!

Just further along the old Earl's Way towards Congleton, on the right hand side, there still stand some of the large stones that used to make up the monument to a fertility goddess. They are now called The Bridestones. And further, on top of the Cloud itself, can be seen traces of what could be an ancient hill fort.

Also, carved in the rock on top of the Cloud there is a sun falling out of the sky. It could have something to do with the double sunset seen over the Cloud.

The Bridestones – a relic of the fertility goddess

Take the Congleton road off the A523 Macclesfield to Leek road. Beyond the crossroads for Bosley Cloud, The Bridestones residence on the right. The Bridesstones can be seen, and a marked footpath leads to them.

The Bridestones is one of the few long barrows found in Britain with a paved forecourt. The Bridestones, or Bridlestones as they are sometimes known, derive their name from St Bride which is yet another Christianised form of a pagan name – *Brigit* – the fertility goddess of the Brigantes, a tribe more usually associated with the area north of the Mersey or Maeres-ea "boundary river".

What can be seen now is only a small part of what used to be there. In 1764, for instance, we know that "several hundred loads" of stones were taken from the site for making a turnpike road about 60 yards away.

Briefly, what can be seen now is a chamber with two large upright stones and a number of smaller stones dotted around. Undoubtedly there have been burials there and undoubtedly the whole at one time formed a stone circle of quite large proportions.

Equally certain is that this area had immense religious significance to our ancestors for not far away there is an ancient cemetery in a corner of a field off Dial Lane. This name comes from the Gaelic "deiseil" or "deasil" which means the sunwise direction used in rituals, or south and to the right. To go the other way was to go "widdershins" which is against the course, or anticlockwise.

The ancients never passed a burial ground or a religious site while walking "widdershins". Often they had to walk three times around a site in the correct manner – sunwise.

A Fort or not?

There is now a conflict of opinion as to whether there was a hill fort on The Cloud, or, to be more precise, at Cloud End. Sainter described it in 1878 as "the remains of a British Hill Fort with its unusual rampart and fosse". He said what was left was in an oblique curve 790 feet long and there was another part to the south 180 feet long.The trench was dug out of solid stone and it has been suggested the area was known as the "Cat Stones" which in Celtic meant the place of battle or "site of graves".

How Dr Sainter thought the Bridestones would have looked before they were desecrated, in his book "Scientific Ramblings around Macclesfield".

The Bridestones from Dr Sainter's late 19th century treatise

However, in 1962 on the Ordnance Survey Record Card, J H White said the earthworks were part of a "comparatively modern field system" and in the "History of Congleton" published for the town's Charter Year it was suggested the earthworks were really a plantation enclosure.

One thing is for certain – that site on The Cloud was too important strategically for it not to have been used by our forefathers for something. And I don't think it was for a plantation at that height.

Gun Hill

From Macclesfield to Leek, on the A523, fork left at the Royal Oak, Rushton, then third left on a road signposted to Swythamley and Meerbrook. Turn right at Staggered crossroads. Gun is about half a mile. Alternatively, drive north for Meerbrook village.

From Bosley Cloud can be seen many landmarks. One of them is a hill called Gun, just north of Leek and on the old Leek to Macclesfield route.

This high and bleak hill is a bit of an enigma. It has been the scene of public hangings and, indeed, the last person to be hanged for murder in public, in these parts, was John Naden who swung from the gib at Gun.

A theory was put forward at one time that there used to be a hill fort on top of Gun and it was part of a line of forts built by the Romans. There was certainly a "square entrenchment" to be found there at some point in the more recent past.

The theory went that a line of hill forts was built by the Romans between the rivers Dove and Severn after Ostorius Scapula's campaign of AD 50 and this line formed the "Limes Britannicus", a supposed chain of stations with a connecting road and an occasional raised earthwork of wall for further defence.

There is certainly a standing stone on the hill which could have been a marker for the old road – or part of an ancient fort?

Murder at Gun Hill

Gun Hill has a local legend which may, or may not be true. It is said to be the place from which Oliver Cromwell's troops fired a cannon at St Edward's Church at Leek. Where the cannonball hit the spire, it is said, a hole was made just off-centre and later a clock was installed into this, which is why it is not in the centre of the spire today. This is sometimes put forward, quite wrongly, as why the area is known as Gun.

Gun stands on the ancient trackway between Macclesfield and Leek and the crossroads are where felons and murderers were hanged. Certainly there are many districts wherein crossroads were the places of hangings. Souls could not find their way, it was supposed, and these meeting points of tracks often had earth powers associated with them as well. Nevertheless, the site of Gun as a gallows field poses one obvious question – Why was it used for that purpose, being so far out of the town? The logical answer is that it was used long before Leek was an important centre which begs the theory that the area we now know as Gun was far more important at one time that it is today.

The last person to be hanged, in chains, from the gallows at Gun was John Naden on Tuesday 31st August, 1731. Naden had murdered his master, a farmer at a place called Whitelea, and it appeared he had been put up to it by the farmer's wife with the promise of her favours.

At the execution of Naden, on Gun Hill, a large concourse of people gathered to witness it, the choir of the Leek parish church and many others from Nonconformist chapels of the district also attended and sang a hymn. No doubt there was much drunkenness at the hanging – it was a good excuse for the worthy townsfolk to see justice was done and to "make an occasion" of it as well.

A stone pillar at Gun

Alderley Edge: Seeking the Grail

On the Macclesfield to Alderley Edge road by the Wizard Hotel

Few can doubt that one of the most romantic and mystical sites in the entire area is The Edge at Alderley. The legend of Merlin and the sleeping knights and the Hallowe'en witches are two of the main reasons but the walks in the leafy glades and the magnificent views over the Cheshire Plain add to the atmosphere.

The Celts and the Saxons found this a special place and the Romans certainly used it. Today, the Merlin legend has been a trifle stretched and commercialised and the witches have been frightened away.

The name "Alderley" itself shows the area once had special significance in a mystical sense because the alder tree, sometimes known as the eller tree, was sacred in northern regions of England. Undoubtedly alder trees abounded at one time, hence the name and there is an ancient game for children sometimes called "The Eller Tree" where kiddies danced around the tallest of their group, preferably a girl and then jumped in trying to tread on each other's toes. This act of circling, sunwise, around a sacred object, whether it be a tree like the alder or a standing stone or stone circle was with us before the Roman invasion.

Witches left The Edge in the early 1960s after a local newspaper carried pictures of them clad in white robes and walking, sunwise, around the large fire. This Coven, from Manchester, left the area because of the huge glare of publicity that ensued.

Yet still the Edge is invaded by hundreds upon hundreds of people at Hallowe'en. Many wear masks or costumes and some make a great deal of noise. Police have to work overtime to keep the peace in this ritual which is still being re-lived in a similar manner to how it was countless hundreds of years ago.

Nearly 200 years ago someone built a circle of stones on The Edge and called it a Druid's Circle. For what reason we do not know, but the circle can still be seen.

It has no significance whatsoever to the powers of the Edge. It's a red herring!

Because of the Edge's height and its position there is no doubt it has been used as a beacon site for countless years. The first actual record we have of it is on the earliest map of Cheshire, that of Saxton in 1578. The old beacon was described as a "hollow square room with a door and having an iron pot kept in it for the purpose of holding pitch and tar".

"Castle Rock" is so named because the Earl of Chester's masons once decided to build a castle there. There is evidence still of foundations on the uncompleted site but there is a big question mark as to why the castle was begun and not finished. Beeston Castle further to the west is strategically excellent for Cheshire's defence against the Welsh. Also, there are wonderful views around all the points of the compass from there. The Earl and his advisors knew why they wanted to build a castle on the Edge before work on it was begun. It was only after foundations were laid that the site was abandoned.

Masons in those far off times were a select band of men who keep secrets and handed them down from father to son. Those secrets were not only concerned with the act of building wonderful buildings like castles and cathedrals but also WHERE to build them. The sites were as important as the construction and often sites would be selected because of those dragon lines, or earth energies, we have alluded to previously.

These lines can be interrupted, particularly by quarrying, and their positive powers can turn negative.

There was quarrying on the Edge, particularly for copper, before the Normans arrive. Could this be a reason?

The Wizard

Of course, the Edge's main claim to fame today is the Legend of the Wizard. I am sure most people have heard it but just in case there are some who have not, I will relate the original story as told in Earwaker's "East Cheshire".

A farmer from Mobberley, whilst crossing the Edge on his way to Macclesfield, having with him a milk-white steed, was accosted by an old man dressed in dark flowing gown who offered him a price for the horse which the farmer refused. The old man then said that no purchaser would be forthcoming at Macclesfield but that on the farmer's return he would again meet him and purchase the animal. As he had been forewarned, no offer was made for the horse, and, returning with it towards Mobberley, he was once again accosted by the old man who ordered him to follow and let the way towards a rock, which he struck, whereupon it opened disclosing a massive pair of iron gates at the entrance to a deep cavern. The gates flew open with a terrible noise and the farmer fell on his knees and besought the wizard to spare his life. He was then taken into the cavern where he saw a countless number of men and milk-white steeds, all fast asleep. After being paid for his horse the wizard told him that a day would come when these men and horses would come forth and would decide the fate of a great battle and save their country and till that date no-one would ever behold the iron gates again.

The Wizard, formerly called the Miner's Arms. This is how it looked before the second world war

This legend was first published in a paper called the Manchester Mail in 1805 and was then said to have been "collected from the tradition of the neighbourhood and some slight-written documents but chiefly from the report of a very old man, Thomas Broadhurst". It added the story was told by Parson Shrigley former clerk and late curate of Alderley who died in 1776 "generally believed by all the neighbouring peasantry".

The same year that the newspaper published this report, the Coach and Horses at Monks Heath changed its name to the Iron Gates. The Miners Arms on the Edge road later changed its name to the Wizard.

Originally the story did not refer to King Arthur. He was brought in to it by James Roscoe a native of Warrington and then a resident of Knutsford whose version was published in Blackwoods Magazine in February, 1839.

This legend is not exclusive to The Edge, I'm afraid.

At Cadbury Castle in Somerset, legends say that once every seven years a door in the hillside opens to let King Arthur and his knights come out to water their horses.

An ancient mound in Marlborough College grounds, Wiltshire, which is supposedly Merlin's burial place, has a similar story.

Merlin is supposed to be lying waiting for Britain's darkest hour in Merlin's Cave, Carmarthen while Arthur sleeps in a cave near Glyn Neath, Glamorgan.

In Scotland he and the knights sleep in the Eldon Hills near Melrose.

What is significant about the Cheshire legend is not sleeping knights or the wizard but the references to the white horses. The white horse was a sacred Celtic animal. A legend concerning the white horse of Uffington, that figure cut out of the chalk hills, has the white horse related to earth energy and there was a strong Celtic horse-cult wherein Celtic kings were symbolically born from a white mare at their coronation. The goddess Rhiannon took the form of a white horse.

Is this legend of the power under the earth a remnant of the Earth Rites of the religion of old?

Celtic and pre-Celtic initiates said there were powerful centres in certain parts of these islands of ours (and on the European Continent) known only to the Chosen Ones (the Holy Men) and these "chakras" lie underground waiting to the released by those with the knowledge of power.

Arthur was the only one with the power to release Excalibur. That sword was, said our forebearers, that earth energy. Traditions handed down refer to a number of places throughout the country where these powers lie buried.

Is the Edge one of them?

Excalibur is the sacred sword and the tribe of the Tuatha de Danaas who gave their name to the Rivers Dane and Dean and Danes Moss had a sacred sword. Excalibur is Merlin's power and Merlin the Wizard is the magical force venerated by the Celts.

Does this legend, therefore, refer to this?

The supposed Druid's Circle on The Edge. There are no earth lines registered around it, and it is assumed it was created comparatively recently as a "folly" or as someone's whimsy.

The Old Straight Track of the White Monks

See sketch map of Viewing Points for directions

In previous chapters I have referred to the earth energy lines, the siting of religious centres and the Old Knowledge.

I would like to relate what I feel is proof positive of these matters in this concluding part. My son Charles and a good friend Mike Oldham traced a line of power from the Parish Church at Leek through the high altar of the now demolished Dieulacresse Abbey, over Shutlingslowe Hill, through Macclesfield Forest Chapel to a tumulus at Rainow where we found, exactly at the centre of the tumulus, a winter wreath in a small circle of stones. As a slight detour, we investigated the Hermit's Cave close to the Abbey Site and discovered, among other things, that there had been buildings around the cave at one time.

I must emphasise that both the sites of the Hermit's Cave and of the Abbey are on private property and must not be visited unless permission is obtained from the owners at Abbey Farm. The site of the tumulus at Rainow is, likewise, in a field which is private property.

Our journey was guided by dowsing or divining rods – instruments used for countless hundreds of years by road builders, master masons and quite simply, anyone attuned to the earth.

We had heard the tales of secret passages going from Leek's ancient church to the Abbey almost due north.

Gateway at Dieulacresse Abbey Farm

There are many of these tales in many towns (Macclesfield has many concerning the Parish Church and the Castle). Our assumption was that these passages could have been energy lines, nowadays referred to as ley lines.

The journey began on a frosty October day in 1986 when we arrived at the rear of the Parish Church of St Edward the Confessor and paraded up and down with "the rods" to find if there was any energy lines flowing to or from the church. There was one, a very powerful line, and it flowed in the general direction of the Abbey.

Off we went across the Park at the rear of the Church following this line which was a "positive and negative" flow measuring up to 70 feet in width. It took us across Fowlchurch, a council-owned tip which (as its name implies) was once where the monks kept their fowl and down into the valley where the Abbey was built.

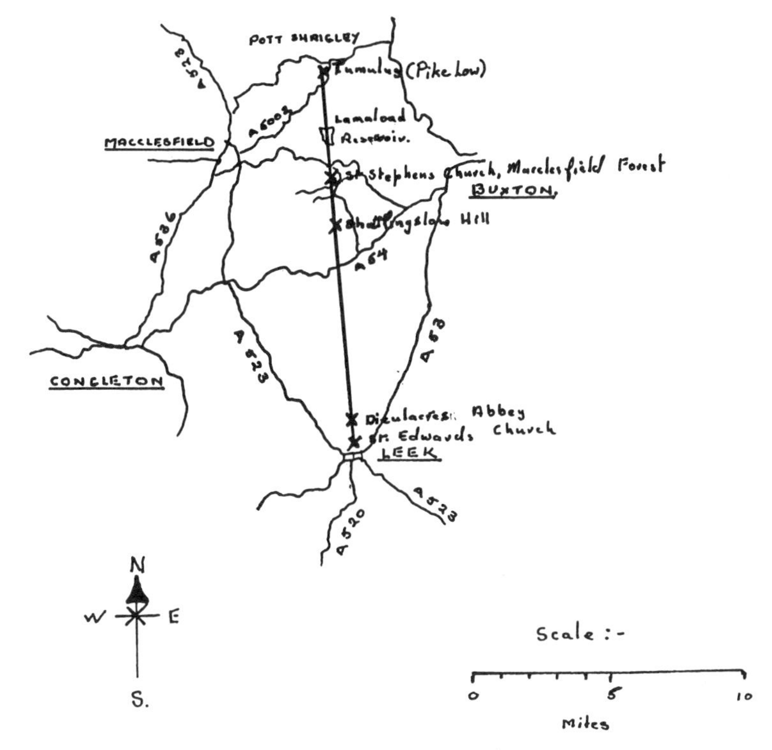

Sketch Plan Showing Line of Ley

After seeking permission from the owners of the site we made our way along this energy line to the field where the Abbey once stood.

Very little remains of this Cistercian site where the White Monks came at the behest of their patron, the Earl of Chester, who brought them there to escape the pillaging Welsh. They founded their Abbey near a site where an Anchorite or Hermit had lived in a cave.

It is a relatively easy task to dowse in the open field for where the abbey walls had been and in the space of one morning the three of us had marked out and mapped the size and shape of the Abbey.

We decided to explore the Hermit's Cave a short walk away and made some interesting discoveries there. It obviously was a much bigger cave at one time, for there is now a lot of debris and dust on the floor making the ceiling lower than it used to be. There were some interesting markings on the ceilings (reproduced in this book) and holes and markings at the front of the cave where there were, presumably, some form of buildings at one time.

An hour's work with the divining rods showed the size and shape of and layout of whatever buildings had been there at one time. Were they, perhaps, a chapel before the monks arrived?

It was quite a common occurrence for a holy man to be blocked up in a cave or shrine, with only enough of an opening for his face to be seen and food and water to be passed through. His or her visitors, mainly for healing purposes, would have first of all entered a chapel.

Returning to the site of the Abbey, we found that the energy lines did some pretty strange things at the point where (if our dowsing rods were telling the truth) the high altar would have been. The energy seemed to go round and round like water going down a plughole. We spent over half an hour standing at this spot. It seemed like only two minutes.

Off we went again, following this fascinating line. We went over Gun Hill and on to Shutlingslow. Shutlingslow Hill, 1,661 feet above sea level takes its name from a pre-Roman tribe of Britons called the Scythingas who also gave their name to Shutlington in Warwickshire and Shuttlestone in Derbyshire. We trudged up the hill and our dowsing on the top showed there was a grid of ley-lines criss-crossing its flat top.

Off we went again and our line took us to St Stephens Church in Macclesfield Forest. We continued northward and came to Lamaload Reservoir, built this century. The line went through it but, not wishing to be the first to try underwater dowsing, we skirted around and picked the line up again on the other side.

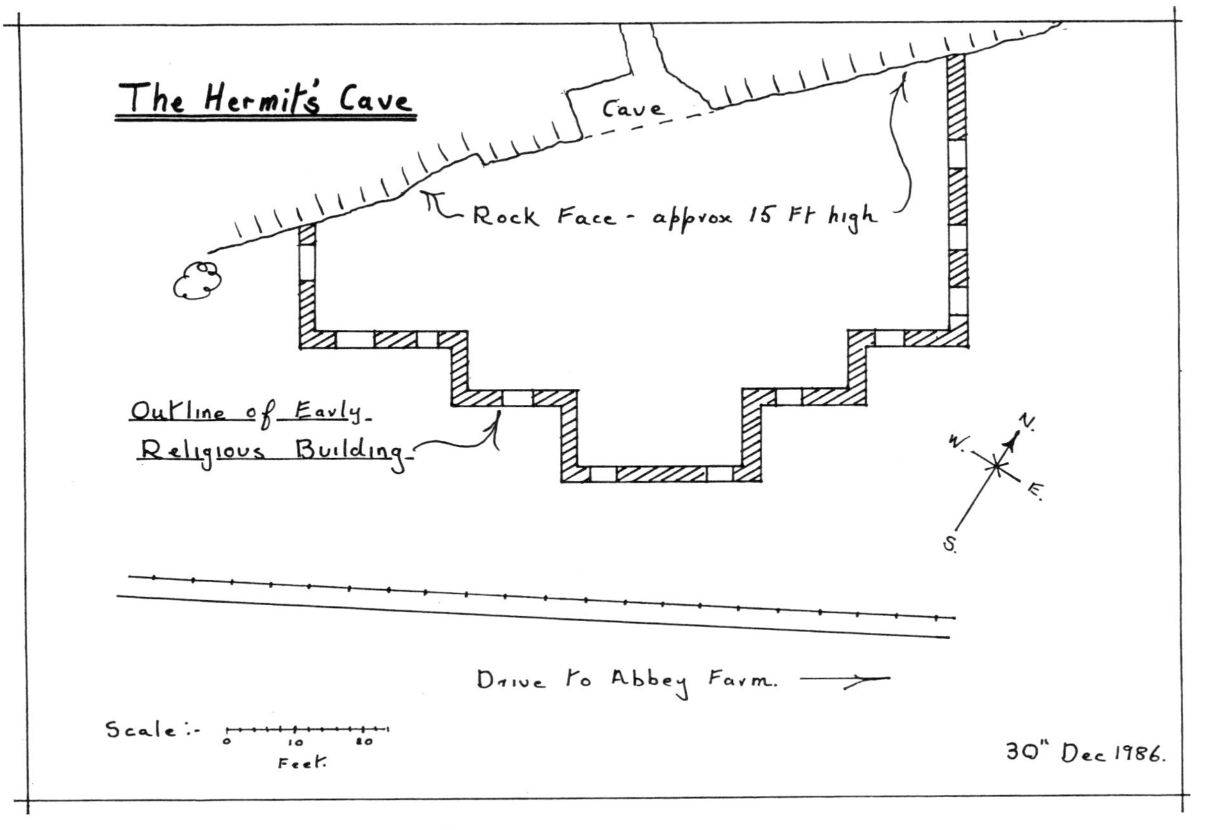

The Hermit's Cave

Markings on the roof of the Hermit's Cave at Dieulacresse

Over towards Rainow, we passed Blue Boar Farm and climbed up a steep hill where a clump of trees could clearly be seen on the summit. When we reached the top a circle of stones was evident among the trees and our line took us to the centre of this circle. The "plug hole effect" was noticeable again and we came across a small circle of stones at this spot.

In the middle was a freshly made wreath.

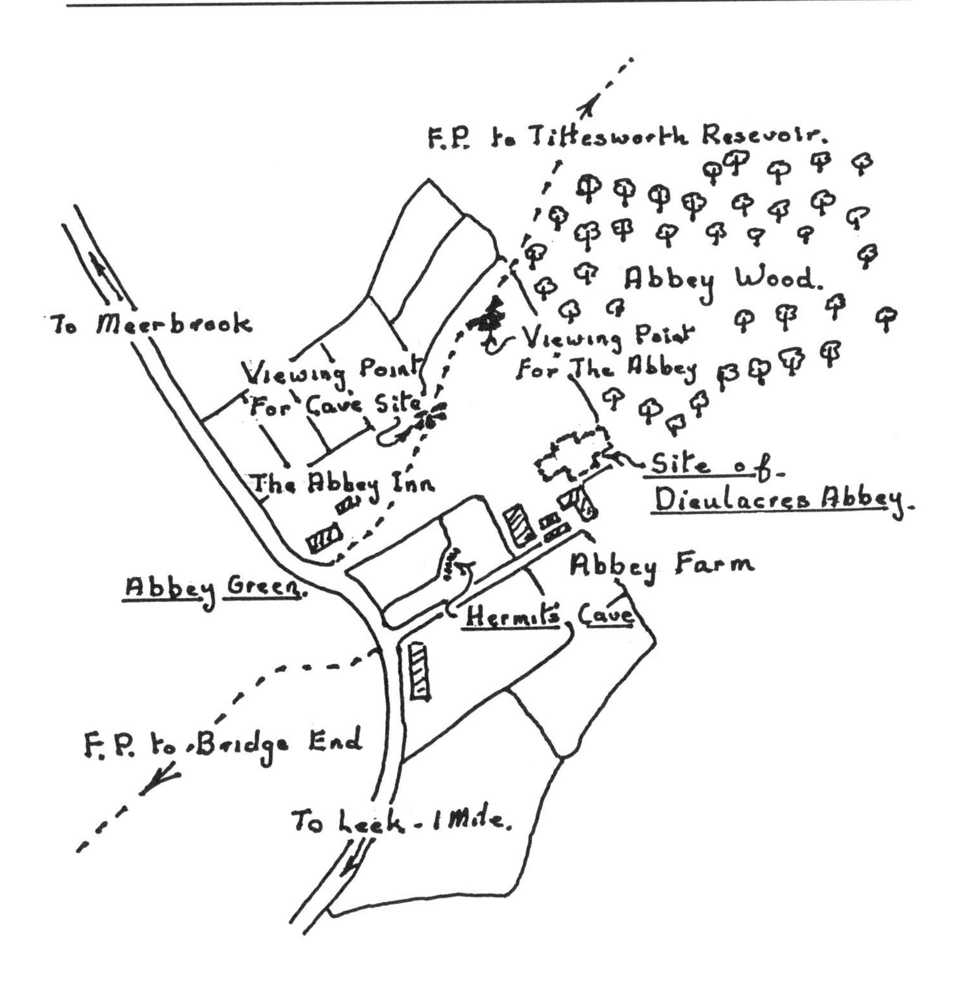

Sketch Plan Showing Viewing Points on Public Footpath above Abbey and Cave Sites.

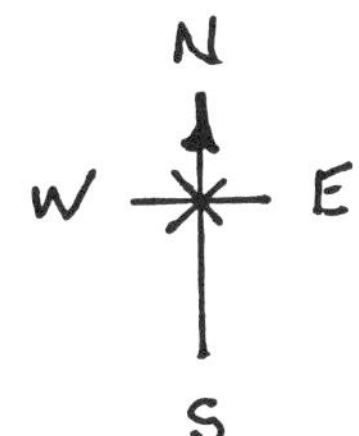

Viewing Points of Abbey Site

The start of the journey at the rear of the Parish Church at Leek

Dowsing at the site of the Abbey

The mouth of the Hermit's Cave

Unexplained markings at the Hermit's Cave. Is the top one the Evil Eye, or is it the serpent symbol? Below: Similar markings to this can be found at Bosley Cloud.

Inside the Cave of the Hermit

Journey's end...what we found at the end of the Ley Line

INDEX